BATS IN THE BELFRY

Bats in the Belfry

MURRAY WATTS

with cartoons by the author

MINSTREL

Eastbourne

A royalty from each copy sold of this book goes to the
work of the Children's Society. For information about
the Society, see page 149.

Cover illustrations by Norman Stone

British Library Cataloguing in Publication Data

Watts, Murray
  Bats in the belfry.
  I. 'Title
  828'.91407

  ISBN 1-85424-008-0 (Minstrel)
  ISBN 0-7324-0430-1 (Albatross)

Co-published in Australia by
Albatross Books, PO Box 320, Sutherland NSW 2232

Printed in Great Britain for
Minstrel, an imprint of Monarch Publications Ltd
1 St Anne's Road, Eastbourne, E Sussex BN21 3UN by
Richard Clay Ltd, Bungay, Suffolk
Typeset by Nuprint Ltd, Harpenden, Herts AL5 4SE.

For Simon Watts

Acknowledgements

Many people have told me jokes, not just for this book but throughout my life, and I cannot begin to remember or thank them all. However, I will thank my father, who gave me my first taste of religious jokes.

Second only to his influence must be Paul Burbridge, my life-long friend and fellow-conspirator, who has made a number of excellent suggestions for this book. My cousin, Andrew Watts, and I had marathon joke sessions years ago, and there must be some of his inspiration here. *Bats in the Belfry* is fittingly dedicated to his son Simon, my god-son.

Other friends have been a great influence on me, not least Canon Raymond Hockley and the late Canon David Watson, both of whom were acknowledged in my last book. A few items in *Bats in the Belfry* were first told me by them. I am very grateful to Norman Stone for another brilliant cover cartoon, and my friends and family at St John's Methodist Church, Sutton-in-Ashfield, who gave me valuable suggestions and encouragement. My thanks too to one of the most originally funny writers around, Adrian Plass, for his suggestions. Among many others who suggested material, Alfredo Michelsen, the best raconteur I know, gave me some memorable stories, and the Revd Charlie Cleverly, famous for illustrating his Sunday morning joke-telling sessions with fine sermons, was an indispensable consultant.

Thank you above all to the Revd John Dixon who sent the following items to me: 7, 74, 75, 82, 85, 91, 94, 95, 96, 97, 98, 102, 156, 159, 167, 169, 209, 211. These were principally from his Major Chuckle column and some from his article on humour, published by *Third Way* Magazine. A number of John Dixon's contributions were from other sources, which are mentioned accordingly, but I would particularly like to acknowledge the Rosamund Essex column in the *Church Times* for the Major Chuckle entries which have gone into the Priceless Pearls chapter. The contributor of some of these items to the *Church Times* was the Revd Leo Morris. I am elsewhere indebted in this chapter to the pioneering collections of schoolboy howlers first made by Cecil Hunt over fifty years ago, and then published by John Lane and Methuen. Even howlers and quotations, which appear at specific moments in time, take on a proverbial air; but jokes, especially, float on the ether for so many years and in so many permutations that it is impossible to trace the original sources. I suppose there may be some gnome somewhere, who sits in a subterranean joke-factory, inventing all these stories which pour into the stream of human consciousness, and, if so, I'd like to thank him.

My heartfelt thanks to my friend and paragon of an editor, Tony Collins, who made this book possible. Finally, I'd like to thank my wife Julie, who kept me insane throughout the preparation of the manuscript. She has the best sense of humour I know. And she needs it.

Contents

Introduction

I am delighted to have *Bats in the Belfry* associated with The Children's Society. The Society does a remarkable work and needs increasing support in a world where many families are under threat. I have never met a child without a sense of humour, but I have met many adults who have lost their ability to laugh along the thorny path to 'maturity'. Children need protecting and their natural gifts, which include humour, need cultivating in an environment of love—and this is the essence of the Society's work.

This year The Children's Society celebrates its centenary in Wales. Living there and having two children of my own are further motives for continuing the link that was established with *Rolling in the Aisles*.

The popularity of *Rolling in the Aisles*, came as a surprise to me. Perhaps I underestimated the importance of humour in the lives of so many people and so many churches, not to mention the enthusiastic advocacy of booksellers throughout Britain. I am grateful for all the encouragement, and *Bats in the Belfry* is my response.

Murray Watts
Easter 1989

THE
ALTERNATIVE
CHURCH GUIDE

The Good Church Guide has been published recently. Names, locations and descriptions of churches are given, with little symbols indicating size of congregation, liturgical usage, length of sermons, musical style. The temptation to publish an alternative guide is overwhelming: strength of tea served in church hall, average temperature of nave in February, diseases of church cat, precise number of eligible single people, sell-by date of biscuits sold at coffee mornings, likelihood of vicar being converted...

Failing such an exhaustive survey, these stories will have to do for the first edition.

1 There had always been mutual hostility between the members of the 'Pure and Simple Faith Baptist Movement' and the rival sect in town, 'The Only True Original Baptist Church of the New Testament'. The elders of the respective chapels never spoke to each other, but on one occasion an elder who had dangerously moderate leanings decided to try and start a conversation. He nodded at an elder from 'The Only True Origi-

nal' sect and remarked: 'I passed your chapel the other day.'

'Thanks,' came back the reply, 'I appreciate it.'

2 A little girl was on her first visit to church, where she saw the congregation kneeling down to pray.

'What are they doing, Mummy?' she asked. 'They're praying, dear.'

'Praying?' She began to giggle. 'What, with all their clothes on!?'

3 A man arrived at the vicarage and was met by the teenage son.

'I'm sorry, my father's busy at the moment—he's just had a phone call offering him an industrial chaplaincy.'

'But he's only been here two years.'

'I know. But he'd get a new car, a big house and a huge salary.'

'What's he going to do?'

'Don't know. He's in the study praying for guidance.'

'And your mother?'

'Oh, she's upstairs packing.'

4 A motorist was walking from the phone box to his car when he stopped a passer-by:

'Excuse me, does anyone in this village own a large black dog with a white collar?' The man shook his head.

'Definitely no dogs of that description round here, mate.'

'In that case,' said the motorist, 'could you lend me 10p? I'll have to ring the RSPCA and tell them not to bother—it was only the vicar I ran over.'

5 The story is told of a British ambassador nervously attending his first official function in Austria. Hundreds of diplomats and society figures were there: it was a truly magnificent event. The food was exquisitely prepared, rare vintage wines flowed freely, the orchestra played brilliantly. The atmosphere of the occasion was overpowering and he was swept along, forgetting his nerves. He turned to the woman next to him, who was wearing a beautiful red dress encrusted with jewels, and asked her for a dance. She declined and gave him three reasons.

'First,' she explained, 'this is a banquet, not a ball. Second, the music you are hearing is the Austrian National Anthem. And third, I am the Cardinal Archbishop of Vienna.'

6 The organist in the little gospel hall had struggled through a number of hymns, valiantly but not very successfully, when the preacher whispered to him:

'Can't you play anything more up-to-date?' The organist whispered back:

'You can't have anything more up-to-date than this— I'm making it up as I go along.'

7 One enterprising Christian magazine ran a competition to see who could find the corniest church notice board. A popular one is: CH..CH—WHAT'S MISSING? U R. Another warns: SEVEN PRAYERLESS DAYS MAKE ONE WEAK. One church claimed to be the SOUL AGENTS FOR THE DISTRICT.

(Quoted in the magazine Ship of Fools, *edited by Simon Jenkins.)*

8 A high churchman was in the habit of dating his letters to the bishop: 'Candlemas', 'St Stephen's Day,' 'The Feast of St Barnabas', 'All Saints Day.' The bishop, a mild man of low church persuasion, became increasingly irritated by this. Finally, on receiving a letter headed: 'Holy Innocents' Day, St Stephens's Rectory', he replied: 'Washing Day, the Palace.'

9 A rural dean was carrying out his duty of inspecting local churches, to see if they were in good condition. He arrived at a little village church where the door was hanging off its hinges, hymn books and prayer books were falling apart, the carpets frayed and threadbare, kneelers losing their stuffing, and the pews battered and scratched. He reprimanded the verger:

'You should see my church. It's in perfect order, spotless!'

'Well, you have an unfair advantage—no one comes into your church,' said the verger.

10 A Welshman was stranded on a desert island for twenty years. At last he was rescued by a merchant ship blown off-course during a storm. Arriving on the island, the sailors were amazed to see that the Welshman had not only built himself a finely constructed timber house, but a village with all sorts of amenities. There was a shop, a hall, a drinking fountain—and two chapels.

'What's the other chapel for?' they asked.

The Welshman replied sternly: 'That's the one I don't go to.'

11 A clergyman was sitting on a bench in Trafalgar Square, eating his lunch, when a man in a grubby raincoat came up to him.

'Naughty postcards, Vicar?'

'Kindly go away,' said the clergyman. The man looked around shiftily, then whispered:

'Naughty but nice, Vicar, eh, lovely postcards, bit of what yer fancy—'

'My dear man,' spluttered the clergyman, 'please leave me in peace to eat my lunch.'

But the man was not to be put off.

'Oh, go on, Vicar, naughty postcards, under the counter, bit of all right, eh, eh, very cheeky postcards, Vicar.'

'Oh, very well,' the clergyman sighed angrily, taking a bundle out of his pocket, 'how many do you want?'

12 I can still remember the Latin grace that I had to recite at college—but not what it meant. I sympathise with the panic-stricken vicar who, faced with a *'Dominus vobiscum'* from his bishop, murmured the reply: *'Er...et tu, Brute!'*

That is a true story, but I cannot vouch for the following:

13 A clergyman, who suffered from classical illiteracy, was asked to say grace in Latin at an Oxford college and seized on the impressive sequence: *'Omo lux domestos brobat!'*

14 A very old and extremely deaf man had attended his Methodist church for more than seventy years. Nobody minded his tuneless singing, but his habit of saying 'Amen' loudly five minutes after the prayers had ended—or suddenly in the middle of the notices—was a serious distraction to the worshippers. When at last somebody pointed this out to him, the old man became very embarrassed and decided to come to a secret arrangement with a small boy, who always sat in the balcony overhead. The plan was brilliant. The little boy would bring a bag of dried peas into church, and every time the old man needed to say 'Amen', the boy would drop a pea onto his bald head.

'For thine is the kingdom, the power and the glory, for ever and ever—ping—Amen.'

The system was apparently foolproof, and the congregation was none the wiser—just impressed that the old man's hearing seemed to be improving. However, the people were astonished one Sunday when, right in the middle of a prayer, the old man shouted: 'Amen-amen-amen-amen-amen-amen-amen-amen-amen-amen!'

And a voice called from the gallery, 'Shut up, you fool, the bag's bust!'

15 Every day, at precisely 10.32 am, the local vicar would leave whatever he was doing and go into his study—from where he could see the Inter-City 125 rush past the bottom of his garden. In the middle of a prayer-meeting, or a planning committee, even during a counselling session, the vicar would get up at 10.32, go into the study, and gaze at the express train as it flashed past. One day, the new curate decided to rebuke him gently: 'Isn't your hobby getting a little out of hand?'

'Oh, I'm not interested in train-spotting,' explained the vicar. 'I just like to see the only thing that moves in the parish without me having to push it.'

16 A member of the True Apostolic Church of Christ the Redeemer in Gobthwaite was boasting about the church's new organ to a member of the schismatic group, the Completely True without a Shadow of Doubt Church of Christ The Supreme Saviour in Gobthwaite and Cleethorpe.

'Now you've got an organ,' said the second man, vastly unimpressed, 'all you'll be needing is a monkey.'

'Well, all you'll be needing,' retorted the other, 'is the organ.'

17 His Holiness the Pope mingled informally with the crowd in St Peter's Square today when the balcony collapsed.

18 One of my favourite true stories was told to me by the Harrison family from Bishop's Stortford. Mrs Harrison was in her garden when the vicar's five-year-old son—a near neighbour—climbed over the wall to see her. She had a pair of shears in her hands and was cutting the hedge.

'What are those?' asked the little boy.

'Shears,' she told him.

'That's what my father says when he's drinking sherry.'

19 A leaflet passed around a theological college in Salisbury suggested the brilliantly original scheme of 'Chain Vicars'. It read:

'If you are unhappy with your vicar, simply have your churchwardens send a copy of this letter to six other churches who are also tired of their vicar. Then bundle up your vicar and send him to the church at the top of the list in the letter. Within a week you will receive 16,435 vicars and one of them should be all right. Have faith in this chain letter and do not break the chain. One church did and got their old vicar back.'

(Quoted in St Paul's Church magazine, Brentwood)

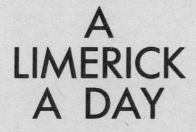

A
LIMERICK
A DAY

A verse to remember for each day is a popular tradition, ranging from anthologies like Daily Light *to photographic calendars with texts. I like the calendars best, especially when the pictures are curiously inappropriate for the words.*

20 One text I saw was, 'I will lead you in the way you should go,' with a picture of a few rotting planks leading into a treacherous marsh on the edge of Lake Windermere.

Here are a few more unhelpful suggestions for meditation.

21 There was a young girl of Shanghai,
Who was so exceedingly shy,
   That undressing at night
   She turned out the light
For fear of the All-Seeing Eye.

(Bertrand Russell)

22 There was an archdeacon who said:
'May I take off my gaiters in bed?'
   But the bishop said: 'No,
   Wherever you go
You must wear them until you are dead!'

23 There once was a pious young priest
Who lived almost wholly on yeast,
   'For,' he said, 'it is plain
   We must all rise again
And I want to get started at least.'

24 A silly young man from the Clyde
In a funeral procession was spied.
   When asked: 'Who is dead?'
   He giggled and said:
'I don't know, I just came for the ride!'

25 There was a young boy in the choir
Whose voice went up hoir and hoir
   Till one Sunday night
   It vanished from sight
And they found it next day on the spoir.

26 There was a young monk of Siberia,
Who of fasting grew wearier and wearier,
   Till at length with a yell,
   He burst from his cell,
And devoured the Father Superior.

27 There was a faith healer of Deal,
Who said 'Although pain isn't real,
   If I sit on a pin
   And it punctures my skin,
I dislike what I fancy I feel.'

29

28 There was an old Fellow of Trinity,
A doctor well versed in Divinity,
    But he took to free thinking
    And then to deep drinking,
And so had to leave the vicinity.

29 There was a kind curate of Kew,
Who kept a large cat in a pew,
    Where he taught it each week
    Alphabetical Greek,
But it never got further than MU.

30 There was a young man of Verona,
Who smoked a King Edward Corona,
    Till he turned very green
    And behaved—well, I mean
Like the whale that had dined upon Jonah.

31 There was a young lady from Kent
Who said that she knew what it meant
    When men asked her to dine
    On oysters and wine;
She knew, oh, she knew! But she went.

32 There once was a man who said, 'God
Must think it exceedingly odd
 If he finds that this tree
 Continues to be
When there's no one about in the Quad.'

(Ronald Knox)

33 A reply to the above:
Dear Sir, your astonishment's odd,
I am always about in the Quad;
 And that's why this tree
 Will continue to be,
Since observed by yours faithfully, GOD.

(Anon)

34 We thought him an absolute lamb,
But when he sat down in the jam
 On taking his seat
 At our Sunday school treat,
We all heard our Vicar say—
 'Stand up while I say grace.'

(Dean Inge)

SERVICE
WITH
A SMILE

In recent years there has been a lot of talk about 'near-death' experiences. I am surprised at the fuss. Some people return miraculously from the brink of death every Sunday of the year. Anyone who has listened to the average sermon will know all about such phenomena: strange dragging sensations, voices far away, tunnels of darkness, then music... 'And now hymn number 36.'

35 The solution is not, as someone has observed, to put more fire into the sermons—but to put more of the sermons into the fire.

36 A Methodist minister was walking down the street when a very well-dressed man ran up to him and shook him by the hand.

'Reverend,' said the man, 'I'll never forget that brilliant sermon on temperance you preached five years ago. How you told us of the poor working man, spending his wages in the pub with his children dressed in rags, while the publican was driving round in a Jaguar with his family in fur coats and dressed in the height of fashion!'

The minister nodded solemnly. 'And did my sermon reform your life?'

'Oh, it did, it did,' said the man, 'transformed it beyond recognition! I decided to become a publican myself.'

37 A vicar was obsessed with organising his sermons to the last syllable. He was an extremely fastidious man, a Filo-fax addict, and always broke up his highly logical discourse into three salient points with sub-headings. When he was appointed to a new church, he asked the church-warden for an honest reaction to his first sermon.

'Three points,' said the old man. 'First, you read it. Second, you read it badly. Third, it wasn't worth reading.'

38 Many a sound sermon has sent people sound asleep.

39 Jonathan Swift surveyed his unpromising congregation and began his sermon: 'There are three kinds of pride—of birth, of riches, and of talents. I shall not speak of the latter, none of you being liable to that abominable vice.'

40 Two church-wardens were comparing the sermons of the vicar and the curate.

'I prefer the curate, myself,' said the first.

'Why's that?'

'Well, he says "In conclusion" and concludes, and the vicar says "Lastly" and lasts.'

41 It was an important day for the little church— the first time in many years that it had been graced by the presence of the bishop. The floral decorations were a picture. The silver candlesticks gleamed on the altar. Villagers poured in to listen respectfully to the great man, rumoured as a possible successor to Canterbury. Only one thing went wrong. A man in the front pew fell asleep during the bishop's sermon. A sidesman, who was sitting behind him and was appalled by this behaviour, hit him on the head with a hymn book.

'Hit me again,' called out the man. 'I can still hear him.'

42 A vicar who was tired of receiving buttons in the collection bag decided to shame the culprits in his congregation. He preached a thunderous sermon on the text: 'Rend your hearts and *not your garments*.'

43 An elderly man had been asked to preach at a little Baptist chapel. Although a well-known figure in the community, he was not a good speaker. His wife was furious:

'Don't you remember the disaster the last time you preached? It was a complete muddle! Fancy speaking about St Jonah the Baptist.'

'Well, dear,' mumbled her husband defensively. 'I knew they were both something to do with water.'

'You'll have to cancel it.'

'I can't. It'll look bad.'

'Not half as bad as you preaching a load of rubbish.'

But the man, who was a former lord mayor, was adamant. He had to keep up appearances.

'There's nothing else for it then. I'll just have to come with you and tell you what to say.'

The old buffer, who was utterly ignorant of the Bible, gratefully agreed. So when the day came, his wife hid in the pulpit and whispered the sermon to him, as loudly as she dared—because he was getting a little deaf.

'Moses was a good man.'

He repeated:

'Moses had a good plan.'

She decided to ignore this and hope for the best.

'He made atonement for the people's sins.'

The old man repeated:

'He made toe ointment for the people's shins.'

At this she lost patience and hissed:

'You silly ass, you've gone and spoilt it all.'
And he repeated:
'And the silly ass went and spilled it all.'

44 Hughie Hughes ran a chip shop business in Mill
Street, Llandulas, in addition to selling fish, fruit
and vegetables or coal from an old converted fire engine.
This was a familiar sight in the village in the 1940s, as
were his street cries of *penwaig* (herring) or *glo* (coal)
depending on which day of the week it was. There was
trouble on one occasion when the rector of the time
decided he no longer wanted to buy his fish from Mr
Hughes. When he called at the rectory with his usual
delivery, the rector said that he did not need any fish as
'I'm having it sent direct from Grimsby in a box'.

After that Hughie Hughes was a notable absentee
from the services at St Cynbryd's Church. When the
rector met him a few weeks later, he said, 'We never see
you in church these days, Mr Hughes.'

'No,' he replied, 'I'm having my sermons now in a
box, direct from the BBC!'

(Reprinted with permission from Llandulas—Heritage of a
village *by Margaret Rawcliffe and Brian Jones)*

45 A minister was in despair at the failure of his sermons. Somehow, he never chose a subject that arrested the congregation, made them sit up, think, change their lives—or at least come up to him afterwards, shake his hand and say: 'What a wonderful sermon, Minister.'

No, unfortunately, those who did not fall asleep during his sermons, sneaked past him at the porch or gave him a limp handshake and a formal, 'Good morning, Reverend.'

Things came to a head one weekend. Trying to prepare his sermon, he stormed out of his study and said to his wife:

'What's the use? I might as well climb into the pulpit and talk about riding bicycles.'

'Don't be absurd,' said his wife.

'Well, why not—it would shake them out of their complacency—a totally unexpected, unusual subject—you never know.'

So 'Riding Bicycles' it was. His wife was very apprehensive, but she went into the crèche, as she did every morning service, leaving her husband to face the congregation alone. But as he climbed the pulpit steps, unknown to her, a far more brilliant idea entered his head.

'Not "Riding Bicycles"—no—that'll never wake them up,' he thought, 'I'll preach on sex. I'll startle the whole congregation and preach a frank, searching, compelling sermon—on SEX!!'

And he did. And it was brilliant. It was funny. It was honest. It was moving. It came from the heart. It was the sermon of his life.

Afterwards, the congregation mobbed him. They came up to him, shook his hand, thanked him for taking the lid off so many problems, for his sympathetic insight.

A woman rushed into the crèche and went up to the minister's wife. 'Your husband was wonderful!' she said. 'You should have heard his sermon. Such a brilliant choice of subject.'

'Really?' said his wife, astonished. 'I thought it was a very odd choice considering he's only done it three times in his life. To be perfectly honest with you—' she whispered confidentially '—the first time he fell over and the second time his hat blew off.'

WISECRACKS

A small phrase can inspire a revolution in thought. Déscartes' famous aphorism, 'I think therefore I am,' is an example. A recent adaptation of the same idea,

46 'I'm pink, therefore I'm Spam,'

is probably less helpful but more entertaining. Here are a few wisecracks which have the virtue of truth and entertainment combined.

47 Beware of a half-truth; you may have got hold of the wrong half.

48 One of the advantages of telling the truth is that you don't have to remember what you said.

49 Of all nonsense, religious nonsense is the most nonsensical.

(Robert Burns)

50 Racial prejudice is a pigment of the imagination.

51 While I cannot be regarded as a pillar, I must be regarded as a buttress of the church, because I support from the outside.

(William Lamb)

52 Christians have burnt each other, quite persuaded
That all the Apostles would have done as they did.

(Byron, Don Juan)

53 The story of God's love lost something in the telling when put across by the Spanish Inquisition.

(Katherine Whitehorn)

54 I despise the superstition of a fanatic, but I love the religion of a man.

(Robert Burns)

55 An atheist is a man with no invisible means of support.

(John Buchan)

56 The only way to succeed in life is to follow the advice you offer to others.

57 There is no spectacle so ridiculous as the British public in one of its periodical fits of morality.

(Lord Macaulay)

58 Many might have attained to wisdom, had they not thought that they had already attained it.

(Seneca)

59 Choose your rut carefully—you'll be in it for the next forty years.

60 We were born originals, let us not die copies.

61 The church is the world's most extraordinary club. The entrance fee is nothing, the annual subscription is everything, and the society has been formed for the benefit of non-members.

ALL
CREATURES
GREAT
AND SMALL

The golden rule for actors is 'never appear with children or animals'. And when both children and animals are involved in any story, the effect is overwhelming.

62 A woman, walking her dog on Clifton Downs in Bristol, met my god-daughter, aged three. She looked at Joanna, who was wearing a pair of blue dungarees, and said to her mother, 'What a lovely little boy.'

Joanna turned straight to the woman's dog and said loudly, 'Hello pussy.'

Here are a few more scene-stealing occasions when animals or children or both are the culprits.

63 A little girl screamed and came running in to her mother:

'There's a tiger in the garden!' The mother jumped up and tore back the curtains. A St Bernard was wandering slowly across the lawn.

'That's not a tiger,' she said, 'that's Billy Smith's dog from over the road. You know perfectly well it isn't a tiger. Go and ask God to forgive you for telling such a lie!'

Obediently, the little girl went upstairs. A few minutes later, she came down smiling.

'Well,' said her mother, 'did you ask God to forgive you for telling lies?'

'Yes,' she replied, 'and God said it was okay.'

'Okay?'

'Yes, God said the first time he saw Billy Smith's dog, he thought it was a tiger, too!'

64 A mother was entertaining guests when her five-year-old son began talking to a fly.

'Do you know that God loves you, little fly?' he asked, gently. Everyone was deeply touched by this.

'And do you love God, little fly?' said the budding St Francis. The boy's mother had tears in her eyes.

'Would you like to go to God, little fly?' the boy persisted. The guests looked at him in admiration.

'Then go to God, little fly!' said the boy and squashed it.

65 The steed bit his master;
  How came this to pass?
He heard the good pastor
  Cry, 'All flesh is grass.'

66 A pious old lady saw a beautiful parrot in the pet-shop window. The owner warned her that the bird had picked up shocking language from its former owner, a merchant seaman, but the old lady insisted that she could curb such filthy habits. Sure enough, on the very first day, the parrot swore—using quite a few words that the old lady had never heard before but knew were dreadfully rude. Immediately, she grabbed the parrot from its perch and shut it in the freezer.

'Stay there for a few minutes,' she told the parrot, 'and perhaps the freezing cold will improve your vocabulary.'

As his eyes grew accustomed to the dark, the parrot noticed a frozen chicken and said: 'I hate to think what words you've been using.'

67 When Balaam the prophet made an ass of himself, the Lord made a prophet of his ass.

(Peter Mackenzie)

68 When you feel down in the mouth, remember that Jonah was too.

69 A woman had a dog which was wildly out of control. No matter how many Good Doggy Training Schools, Perfect Pup Evening Classes or Respectable Rover Correspondence Courses she tried, the dog was unmanageable. One day, a famous Christian healer came to town. She went to his meeting and was deeply impressed. If legs could be lengthened, arthritic joints healed, incurable diseases vanquished, why not a dog trained? She went to the healer and begged him to pray for her dog.

'Leave the dog with me during this mission,' he said, 'and the animal will be spiritually transformed.' A week later she came back and, sure enough, a miracle had occurred. When the preacher said, 'Come,' instead of running off and digging up the neighbour's flower-beds, the dog came; when he said 'Sit,' instead of doing a back-flip through the french windows, the dog sat; and when he said 'Fetch,' instead of collapsing on the ground in a coma, the dog ran after the stick and brought it right back to the feet of the preacher.

'Thank you, thank you,' said the woman, tears of joy in her eyes—but then a worrying thought crossed her mind.

'What if my dog only responds to your voice?'

'Give him a command,' said the preacher, 'anything. I promise you, he'll obey every word!'

'Heel!' she shouted, and the dog sat bolt upright, raised its paw in the air and barked:

'Rise up in the name of the Lord!!'

THE
UNAUTHORISED
VERSION

70 A child, told to learn a passage from the Authorised Version of the Bible, explained to her Scripture teacher that she could not because her family only had 'The Reversed Version' at home. Presumably, this edition starts with Revelation (or more strictly, Noitalever) and ends with Genesis (or Siseneg); or perhaps, more worryingly, it has incidents like the Starving of the Five Thousand, the Lowering of Lazarus, and Goliath hurling David from a sling onto a pile of smooth pebbles.

Most of us feel more at home with the traditional order of events, aptly summed up by this extract from A Woman of No Importance *by Oscar Wilde:*

71 Lord Illingworth: The Book of Life begins with a man and a woman in a garden.

Mrs Allonby: It ends with Revelations.

Here are some more offbeat Bible commentaries.

72 A man was beaten up by gangsters on the road to Jericho. He lay there, half dead, robbed of all his money, groaning in agony. A priest came along and passed by on the other side. A Levite came along and passed by on the other side. Finally, a social worker came along, looked at the man and said:

'Whoever did this needs help.'

73 The curate's wife was wearing a very low-cut dress at the Christmas party.

'I see you're wearing a biblical robe tonight,' said a male admirer.

'Biblical?'

'Well, sort of "Low and Behold!"'

74 A doctor, an architect and a politician were discussing whose profession was the oldest. The doctor argued that his was the oldest since God performed a surgical operation when he created Eve out of Adam's rib. The architect claimed that his profession was still older since God, like any architect, in creating the world, made it out of chaos.

'Yes,' said the politician, 'but who do you think made the chaos?'

(from the Major Chuckle column, edited by John Dixon, quoting So You Want to be Prime Minister by Des Wilson, Penguin Books.)

75 A recent correspondent to the *Guardian* newspaper wrote, 'I am glad to see that Mrs Thatcher feels able to say that Jesus "got it about right" with his injunction to "render unto Caesar", etc.'

The writer compared her remark to that of Field Marshall Lord Montgomery who was reported to have started his reading of the lesson at Matins one Sunday with the words:

'And the Lord said unto Moses—and, in my opinion, quite rightly—'

(Letter to The Guardian *from Norman Broadbridge of Chichester, cited in* Buzz Magazine, *December 1988.)*

76 When a fellow politician was described to Benjamin Disraeli as 'a self-made man', Disraeli replied: 'I know he is—and he adores his maker.'

77 'You gentiles have taken everything from us,' argued the Jew.

'Like what?' said the Christian.

'Like the Ten Commandments, for a start.'

'We may have taken them,' replied the Christian, 'but you can't possibly accuse us of keeping them!'

78 The Latest Decalogue

Thou shalt have one God only; who
Would be at the expense of two?
No graven images may be
Worshipped, except the currency:
Swear not at all; for, for thy curse
Thine enemy is none the worse:
At church on Sunday to attend
Will serve to keep the world thy friend:
Honour thy parents; that is, all
From whom advancement may befall:
Thou shalt not kill; but need'st not strive
Officiously to keep alive:

Do not adultery commit;
Advantage rarely comes of it:
Thou shalt not steal; an empty feat,
When it's so lucrative to cheat:
Bear not false witness; let the lie
Have time on its own wings to fly:
Thou shalt not covet, but tradition
Approves all forms of competition.

(Arthur Hugh Clough, 1819–1861)

79 Joshua and Caleb returned from Canaan, saying it was a land 'flowing with milk and honey', and brought back a bunch of grapes to prove it.

80 Why was Goliath so surprised when David hit him with a stone? Because nothing like this had ever entered his mind before.

81 When was the first case of constipation in the Bible? When Moses took the tablets and went into the wilderness.

82 The following lines are quoted from a children's nativity play:

Mary and Joseph approach the innkeeper who tells them there is no room in the inn.

Joseph: But my wife is pregnant.

Innkeeper: Well, it's not my fault.

Joseph: It's not my fault either!

83 A system of ethics has been drawn from the poetry of Byron 'in which the two great commandments are, to hate your neighbour, and to love your neighbour's wife'.

(Lord Macaulay)

84 The rain it raineth on the just
And also on the unjust fella,
But chiefly on the just, because
The unjust steals the just's umbrella.
(Charles, Baron Bowen)

85 A correspondent to *Crusade* magazine condemns the use of the title 'Reverend' as having no scriptural authority. He argues that the Hebrew word *yare* is translated only once as 'reverend' in Psalm 111:9, 'holy and reverend is his name'. Elsewhere it is translated 'terrible', 'dreadfully' and in one instance 'fearfully'.

He suggests that for the title 'Rev', we substitute 'The Terrible'; 'Very Revs' should be addressed as 'The Terribly Dreadful', and 'Right Revs' as 'Fearfully and Terribly Dreadful.'

(Letter from L V Fitz-Gibbon to
Crusade Magazine, *October 1981.)*

PRICELESS
PEARLS

When I was a university lecturer in drama, I had some memorable contributions in the written exams. One student wrote about 'The Duchess of Mafia', another of

86 'Macbeth, Prince of Thermidor' (images of a Scottish warlord doused in a rich cheese sauce).

Writing of the same play, another student wrote:

87 'Even though Macbeth murdered Duncan, it was not wholly for his own edification.'

A second-year student commented sympathetically about Hamlet, 'A rather sad part of the play is the ending,' and one of my fourth-year students, who had attended the honours seminars on tragedy, wrote of King Lear, 'And so we see that all the baddies have died.'

88 However, the essay I treasure most of all was from one girl who, in all charity, I can only describe as a computer error in the admissions policy. Her total contribution, on the subject of the difference between comedy and tragedy, was as follows:

'A tragedy is a true story play it has reality in it. It is contained of the truth. The tragic heroes. They are so called because they are brave, they fight continueally until they conquere. There is seriousness and bravery in a tragic play, compared to comedy where you find actors in a bright spirited mood, laughing, having a lot of fun, jumping, talking to each other on stage because of the fun. Sophoclecles is a tragic play.'

I think that says it all.

But the schoolroom, even more than the university, is the home of the howler. Some examples have become famous over the years.

89 'Three shots rang out. Two of the servants fell dead and the other went through his hat.'

90 'Christians are only allowed one wife and this is known as monotony.'

Here is a collection which most teachers could expand indefinitely.

91 Jesus appeared to two disciples behind locked doors as they were walking to Emmaus.

92 A lie is a sin and an abomination in the sight of the Lord, but a very present help in trouble.

93 John the Baptist was beheaded with the Axe of the Apostles.

94 You must love your neighbour even if you hate him.

95 Everyone was pleased when Jesus healed the paralytic man, except Simon who had to pay to have the roof mended.

96 Jesus stood up in the synagogue at Nazareth and read from the Epistle of St Paul.

97 Four men came carrying a parable on a bed.

98 Jesus said to the man at the pool, 'If you are good and get a good job and repent after you are healed, God will heal you.'

99 If someone slaps you turn and let him have another knock and the door shall be opened.

100 Two Jesuits, probably a man and wife, were on the way to Emmaus.

101 The end of the world will mark a turning point in everyone's life.

102 John said it was not awful for you to marry your brother's wife.

103 Question: Write what you know about Elijah.

Answer: All I know about Elijah is that he went for a cruise with a widow.

104 Question: Write what you know about the Last Supper.
Answer: I was away for that. I had measles.

105 Question: What is a vixen?
Answer: A lady vicar.

106 When the servants arrived at Peter's house, he was on the roof braying.

107 Get the hens, Satan.

108 Thy rod and thy staff they come for me.

109 Lead us not into Thames Station.

110 A gargoyle is seen on church towers and people's necks. They come, whether you like it or not.

111 The Pilgrim Fathers were captured by the Giant Despair. They were a big band of Quackers.

112 Moses received the Ten Commandments on two stones, and these he impressed upon the people.

113 There is always a knave in churches to remind you of sin.

114 The chief missile of the Church of England is the Prayer Book.

115 Question: What is the first and greatest Commandment?

Answer: Hang all the law and the prophets.

116 Question: Who lived in the Garden of Eden?

Answer: The Adamses.

117 Question: Explain the phrase 'the quick and the dead'.

Answer: The quick is the man that got out of the way.

118 Jesus cured Peter's mother-in-law, when she was sick of a fever, and Peter swore and went out and wept bitterly.

119 Lay not up for yourselves trousers on earth.

120 Question: What is an unclean spirit?
Answer: A dirty devil.

121 A man came near to the edge of the volcano. He looked over and saw the creator smoking.

122 Jacob, son of Isaac, stole his brother's birthmark.

IN A
WORD

Words have endless possibilities for distortion.

123 The repetition of one chorus has so numbed my mind that, instead of 'Comfort ye, comfort ye my people', I now hear 'Come for tea, come for tea my people'.

124 Then there is the chorus which seems to be borrowed from some disturbing pagan ritual: 'Agad reigns.' Who is Agad? And should we really be worshipping him in an Anglican service?

125 Paul Burbridge tells me of a preacher with a strong German accent who preached an entire sermon on 'Moses and the burning bus'. It was a remarkable scenario, apparently. 'And then God spoke to Moses from the bus....' ('It's the number 52 for Mount Horeb, Moses.')

126 As for misprints, who wouldn't rush to attend the church service advertised in the parish magazine as 'Evensnog'?

Here is some fun with verbal slips, double-entendres and memorable phrases.

127 St Paul, according to the *New English Bible*, says:
'In my letter I wrote that you must have nothing to do with loose livers.'

128 But even this is surpassed by an early edition of *The Living Bible* which tried to find a contemporary idiom for the incident in 1 Samuel Chapter 24, when King Saul went into a cave in order to (in the words of the RSV) 'relieve himself'. Not satisfied with this straightforward euphemism, *The Living Bible* translates it as follows:

'Saul went into the cave to go to the bathroom.'

129 One of my favourite verbal slips was the reader in church who had Jesus commanding the disciples to 'curse the sick'.

130 The title of my Christmas play, *The Tree That Woke Up*, caused some amusing problems for various enquirers at the Riding Lights office. According to the company newsletter:

'We had *The Tree That Grew Up*, *The Tree That Sprang to Life*, *The Tree That Waketh* (the Authorised Version?), *The Tree That Fell Asleep*, *The Tree That Never Woke Up*, *The Tree That Came Alive*. For others, the initial concept proved hardest: *The* Three *That Woke Up*, for instance. But, as always, the prize had to go to those who plunged right in and made a complete blancmange of the whole lot: "I want to order eighteen tickets please, for *The Day the Bush Sprang to Life*." '

131 Overheard at a mission meeting:
'I was depressed earlier in the meeting, but now that it's finished, I feel so much better.'

132 The marriage suffered a setback in 1965 when the husband was killed by the wife.

(New Law Journal)

133 Mothers' Union sale of unwanted items. Please bring your husbands.

(Parish Magazine)

134 Asked to comment on the new campaign, an official of the Lord's Day Observance Society said last night: 'We don't give statements on Sundays.'

(News Chronicle)

135 It's just called 'The Bible' now—we dropped the word 'Holy' to give it a more mass-market appeal.

(Judith Young of Hodder & Stoughton, quoted in The Observer *'Sayings of the Week')*

136 Anyone who has suffered heavy metal music blasting through the night and the pounding of feet in the flat above will see the attraction of the following advert: 'Mayhew and Sons. Funeral Directors. Parties catered for.'

137 In 1976 I was commissioned by Thames Television to write a play for Good Friday. The main character was a 'lollipop man', who—sheltering in a Brixton church during a rainstorm—held an imaginary conversation with people from the past life of the church and, finally, with God himself. A friend's grandmother was told that I had a 'religious' play on television. She switched on, but when she saw the little man holding his 'STOP' sign and chattering away in a broad accent, she assumed that the 'religious' play was on the other side. She duly switched over to watch the epic Biblical film, 'The Greatest Story Ever Told,' in which John Wayne as the Centurion drawls, 'Surely this waaaas the son of Gaaaad.' She thought that I'd written that and said that she enjoyed my play very much.

138 The vicar and his wife had left for a conference abroad, forgetting to give instructions for the banner which was to decorate the hall at the Christmas Carol Concert, the following weekend. The secretary of the Mothers' Union was astonished to receive a telegram from France which read simply:

'UNTO US A SON IS BORN. NINE FEET LONG AND THREE FEET WIDE. REV AND MRS JOHNSON.'

ALL
GOOD
GIFTS

139 Having a 'good head for money' does not mean that you have a bald head with a long slit in the top.

It means being able to handle money efficiently. But who can handle it well? Who can set limits to its power?

140 One extremely rich man, asked what would really satisfy him, replied: 'Just a little more.'

Money has always been a controversial subject for the church—often the lack of it—but in some disastrous cases wealth has been the problem.

141 Tradition has it that Thomas Aquinas was proudly showed round the Vatican treasury. The Pope said to him: 'We can no longer say, "Silver and gold have we none." '

'No,' said Aquinas, 'and we can no longer say, "In the name of Jesus, rise up and walk." '

142 An old miser was at death's door. The local vicar called to see him and, although a virtual stranger, brought him a bowl of fruit and some flowers. Deeply touched, the old man begged the clergyman to pray for his healing.

'Reverend,' he whispered hoarsely, tears filling his eyes at the thought of his selfish and miserly existence, 'if I recover, if God spares me, I promise you £100,000 towards the Church Restoration Fund!'

The vicar gently squeezed the man's hand and promised to pray for him, though hardly expecting him to make it through the night.

Yet the miracle occurred and the old miser recovered to full health. 'Now at last,' the vicar told the PCC, praising God for strengthening his faith, 'our church building will be saved!' But days...weeks...then months passed, and there was no cheque for £100,000 in the post, no envelope stuffed with bank-notes—not even a first instalment—nothing. Eventually, the vicar could take it no longer. He stormed round to the miser's house and demanded: 'What happened to the £100,000 you promised the church?'

The miser stared at him, utterly astonished. 'When did I promise that?'

'When you were sick.'

I promised the *church* the sum of *£100,000*?'

'Yes!'
'Well, that just shows how sick I was!'

143 First Man: I have nothing but praise for our new minister.
Second Man: So I noticed when the collection plate came round.

144 The church treasurer was sorting through the collection—the usual crop of foreign coins, buttons and paper clips—when he came across an 'I Owe Thee' note.

145 An American evangelist once had wires connected to all the seats in his church.

'All those who are willing to give one hundred dollars to God,' he shouted, 'stand up!'

As he said this, he pressed a button and electricity zapped through the seats. There was a tremendous response, but later the sidesman found three dead Scotsmen clinging to their pews.

146 Lord Soper is famous for his street preaching. On one occasion a heckler sneered at him:

'What's it like being a professional Christian?' Lord Soper replied: 'Very much the same as being an amateur, except I don't make so much money.

147 A woman grudgingly dropped a coin into the collection plate, then sat down to listen to the sermon. Afterwards, she complained loudly at the low standard of the preaching. Her seven-year-old son interrupted:

'Well, what can you expect for 5p, Mum?'

148 On the Sunday following the Watchnight Service, the vicar gave out this notice: 'And would the congregation kindly remember that the box marked "For The Sick" is for financial contributions only.'

MATCHPOINT

149 My friend Alfred Bradley, producer and playwright, was holding a party in York, and among the guests was the brilliant comic actor Roy Kinnear, deeply lamented by all who loved him and admired his work. Alfred had been working on a project in Scotland and historical research had brought to light the whimsical piece of information that John Knox—the man famed for his puritanical views and hostility to women—had, in later life, married a sixteen-year-old girl. When he heard this, Roy gave a quizzical smile and mumbled, in his inimitable way, 'Hmmm...Opportunity Knox.'

Matches, and mismatches, have always been good for a laugh, although frequently the humour becomes a little unsettling.

150 Like the old man who was asked if he had ever considered divorce and replied, 'Divorce never, murder often.'

Here are a few more love stories that will not be published by Mills and Boon.

151 The priest intoned solemnly at the wedding service:

'If any man has any just cause or impediment why these two should not be joined together in holy matrimony, ye are to—'

'Yes, I have!'

'Shut up, you're the groom.'

152 Two tear drops were floating down the river of life. The first tear drop said: 'I am from the eye of a girl who lost her man.' The second replied: 'And I am from the eye of the girl who got him.'

153 The vicar's car broke down on the way to the wedding ceremony and he was half an hour late for the service. The wedding party was beginning to panic when he arrived, and he was so embarrassed he never forgot the incident. Fifteen years later, he met the husband at a party and said:

'I'm so sorry about that horrible fright I gave you on your wedding day.'

'So am I,' said the man, 'I've still got her.'

154   Man: They say that people who spend their lives together end up by looking the same.

Woman: Yes, and that's why I'm refusing to marry you.

155 'MAKE LOVE NOT WAR' said the poster. Underneath someone had written: 'I'm married. I do both.'

156 A Notice ran: 'The lodge meeting has been postponed. The wife of the Grand Exalted Invincible Supreme Potentate won't let him come out tonight.'

157
First Woman: Are you married?
Second Woman: Well, I'm engaged—it's as good as being married.
First Woman: Actually, it's better.

158 There are two periods in a man's life when he does not understand a woman—before he's married and after he's married.

JOKING AROUND

One of my favourite misquotes from the Bible is:

159 Jesus said, 'Behold, I will give you a good lawyer for there will be many trials.'

But for many prisoners of conscience, even a trial may be a luxury.

160 South Africa's Minister of Law and Order, Adriaan Vlok, yesterday vigorously defended his government's policy of detaining troublesome political opponents indefinitely and without charge, arguing that 'according to normal law' it was 'not always possible to find them guilty'.

(The Independent, *10th February, 1989*)

161 A situation which brings to mind the notorious Judge Jeffreys, a ruthless and bigoted judge who presided over the 'Bloody Assizes' in the seventeenth century. On one occasion he pointed with his cane to a man in the dock and thundered, 'There is a great rogue at the end of my cane!' The man replied, 'At which end, my Lord?'

Some of these stories, from different parts of the world, illustrate the humour that miraculously survives in such extreme conditions—and the final few tales offer a glimpse of humour and other faiths.

162 A commandant strode down a line of convicts on parade, asking each man the same question.

'What's your crime?'

'I've done nothing, sir, and I've got ten years.' The commandant moved on.

'And what's your crime?'
'Nothing, sir, and I've got twenty years.'
'Lying swine! Nobody in the People's Republic gets more than ten years for nothing!'

> *(Richard Wurmbrand,* In God's Underground,
> *Hodder & Stoughton)*

163 While I was working in Soweto in 1981, I was told of a white woman going into a church near Bloemfontein, in the very heartland of apartheid. She was horrified to see—in this 'whites only' church—a black woman kneeling reverently at the altar rail. She marched up the aisle, shouting: 'Excuse me,' then noticed that the woman was polishing the brass rail with a cloth.

'Thank heavens for that,' she sighed, 'for one awful moment, I thought you were praying.'

164 Russians are convinced that the Garden of Eden must have been in the Soviet Union. It's the only place a man and woman could be naked, with only an apple to eat, and think they were in Paradise.

165 It was rush hour in Leningrad and the bus was packed. Two men were squashed up together and one turned to the other:

'Excuse me,' he whispered, 'Do you work for the KGB?'

'No.'

'Does your wife work for the KGB?'

'No.'

'Do any of your friends or relatives work for the KGB?'

'No!' said the man, getting impatient.

'I do apologise for bothering you like this,' persisted the other, coughing politely, 'but could you possibly tell me if you know anyone who has ever worked for the KGB?'

'For the last time,' said the man, 'I have no connections whatsoever with the KGB!'

'In that case,' replied the first, 'could you move up? You're standing on my foot.'

166 The Nazi commandant stared at the Jewish rabbi.

'I could have you killed,' he told him, a cruel smile spreading across his face, 'taken out and shot.' The rabbi was silent. 'But,' the commandant continued, 'I am a man of compassion. And looking at the forms here, I can see that today is your birthday.' The rabbi remained motionless. 'And to demonstrate my profound compassion, I am going to give you one chance to escape from death. One of my eyes is made of glass and if you can guess correctly which one, you can go free. If you fail, you will die.'

Immediately, the rabbi pointed to the commandant's left eye.

'That one,' he said.

'Incredible!' gasped the commandant. 'The most brilliant surgeon in the world fitted that glass eye and no one has ever been able to tell the difference before. How did you know?'

'Easy,' said the rabbi, 'it's the one with the compassion in it.'

167 A Roman Catholic priest, a Muslim imam and a rabbi were discussing what each of them would do in the event of another great flood sweeping the earth.

'We would pray and trust in God to spare us,' said the priest.

'We would accept our fate as kismet and die in resignation, knowing it to be the will of Allah,' said the Muslim.

But the rabbi said, 'We would learn to live underwater.'

(From the Major Chuckle column, edited by John Dixon, quoting Egan Larsen in Wit as a Weapon: The Political Joke in History, *Fred Miller, 1980.)*

168 Hitler was fond of consulting palmists, clairvoyants, mind-readers, fortune-tellers—anyone who could calm his increasing paranoia about the future of the war. One of the most famous soothsayers in Germany offered to predict the day of his death. Hitler was horrified but intrigued. If he knew the exact day, he could take measures to defend himself.

'You will die,' the seer assured him, 'on a Jewish holiday.'

Hitler went beserk with rage. 'Which one? Which one? Imbecile!' He beat him about the face.

The soothsayer calmly replied: 'Any day you die will be a Jewish holiday.'

169 An extremely learned Jewish maggid travelled from town to town preaching. He loved to invite and answer questions from his congregations.

The maggid's faithful driver always listened intently both to the sermons and the question-and-answer sessions. One day, as they travelled to a village where they had never been before, the driver suggested that by way of an experiment they switch roles.

Intrigued by the idea, the maggid agreed. The driver delivered a fine sermon and easily answered the questions that were thrown at him. But then a question was asked that was so new, so technical and so profound, the driver had no idea how to answer it.

He hesitated only for a moment before thundering, 'I am amazed you should ask me a question so simple. Why, even my driver, a poor, hard-working, uneducated Jew can answer it. Driver!' he shouted to the maggid. 'You heard the question. Answer it!'

(From the Major Chuckle column edited by John Dixon, and told by Leo Roster in The Joys of Yiddish, *Penguin Books.)*

170 A Hindu, a Muslim and a politician were attending a conference. Unfortunately, the hotel was overbooked and the manager explained that there was only one room available with two beds. Apart from that, there was an old barn in the field outside. The Hindu humbly offered to spend the night in the barn, leaving the other two to enjoy the comfortable beds.

But a few minutes after the Muslim and the politician fell asleep, there was a knock at the door. It was the Hindu, deeply apologetic, but there was a cow in the barn and his religious scruples forbade him to spend the night in its company. So the Muslim graciously offered to take his place.

A few more minutes passed and there was another knock on the door. It was the Muslim. There was a pig in the barn and, he regretted profusely, he could not compromise his beliefs by sharing the night with it. So the politician reluctantly gave up his bed and walked off to the barn.

A few minutes later, there was a loud knock at the door. It was the cow and the pig.

171 Canon Raymond Hockley tells me of a memorable response to some Jehovah's Witnesses. His friend, an impressive man with a bushy beard, was taking a shower when the doorbell rang. He seized a flowing white bathrobe and ran to the door.

'Who are you?' he boomed.

'We're Jehovah's Witnesses,' said the two missionaries, holding out their collecting box.

'Well, I'm Jehovah!' he thundered. 'So hand over the takings!'

172 Another original response was the rabbi who, on hearing that Jehovah's Witnesses were at the door, called out:

'Wonderful! Let's hope he wins his case!'

DEAD
FUNNY

Anyone who has read Evelyn Waugh's The Loved One *will be familiar with the American Way of Death—but some cemeteries have advanced a long way since Waugh's satire: they have invented The Talking Gravestone.*

Now, as you wend your way across the burial plots, you are likely to trigger a tape-recorded message: 'Hello. This is Earl Johnson Jr speaking here. Welcome to my grave.' No doubt many of these messages end with: 'Thank you for calling, have a nice day!' or perhaps, 'Have a nice life!'

Here is some graveyard humour from over the centuries, a few famous last moments, and other examples of deadly wit.

173 Beneath this stone in hopes of Zion
Doth lie the landlord of the Lion;
His son keeps on the business still,
Resigned unto the heavenly will.

(Upton-on-Severn)

174 ERECTED TO THE MEMORY OF
J. MAC FARLANE
Drowned in the Water of Leith
BY A FEW AFFECTIONATE FRIENDS

175 Here lies interred the body of Mary Haselton
A young maiden of this town
Virtuously brought up
Who being in the act of prayer
Repeating her vespers
Was instantaneously killed by a flash of
Lightning
August 16 1785

(Bury St Edmunds)

176 Here lies a one-time Fusilier,
Who carried well his pot of beer,
But now, his active service past,
The bier has carried him at last.

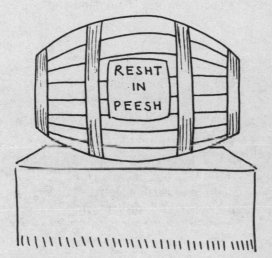

RESHT
IN
PEESH

177 Epitaph for a Dentist

Stranger! Approach this spot with gravity
John Brown is filling his last cavity.

178 Robert Burns wrote the following epitaph for James Grieve, Laird of Boghead:

> Here lies Boghead among the dead,
>   In hopes to get salvation;
> But if such as he, in Heav'n may be,
>   Then welcome, hail! damnation.

179 Here lies, retired from busy scenes,
A first-lieutenant of Marines,
Who lately lived in blithe content,
On board the good ship Diligent.

Now stripped of all his warlike show,
And laid in box of elm below,
Confin'd to earth in narrow borders,
He rises not till further orders.
(From the churchyard of Barwick-in-Helmet)

180 A tombstone, carved in the shape of an open book, has this inscription:

Alfred Halstead, Book Editor
Lent Sept 28th 1852
Returned May 14th 1907
(From a churchyard in Blackpool)

181 Sacred to the memory of Marie (to say nothing of Jane and Martha) Sparks

Stranger, pause and drop a tear,
For Susan Sparks lies buried here:
Mingling in some perplexing manner,
With Jane, Marie, and portions of Hannah.

(Max Adeler)

182 Here lies Mary, the wife of John Ford,
We hope her soul is gone to the Lord;
But if for Hell she has chang'd this life
She had better be there than be John Ford's wife.

(Potterne, Wiltshire)

183 Here lies the body of Jonathan Pound
Who was lost at sea and never found.

184 It has been pointed out that Christians in their prayers often put sick people in the most uncomfortable position, praying for 'those laid on one side'. And if that isn't bad enough they add, 'on a bed of sickness'. And just in case the Lord might be thinking of healing them, they 'beseech the Lord to undertake for them'.

(John Dixon in 'Humour is a Funny Thing',
Third Way Magazine)

185 A sergeant-major was renowned for his blunt approach to life—and death. One morning, shortly before parade, he received a telegram saying: 'Private Hoskins' father has died. Please inform.'

So, as he strutted past the soldiers all lined up for inspection, he suddenly turned to Private Hoskins and shouted, 'Private Hoskins!'

'Sah!' Hoskins saluted.

'Private Hoskins, one pace forward.'

'Sah!' Hoskins stepped forward.

'Private Hoskins, your father is dead. One pace retire. Squad dismiss!'

The army chaplain witnessed this incident, which sure enough had a traumatic effect on Hoskins. He reprimanded the RSM.

'For goodness' sake, man, use some diplomacy next

time. Bereavement needs to be handled with considera-
tion, sensitivity!' The sergeant-major promised to be
more delicate in future. As it happened, it wasn't long
before another telegram arrived, announcing the tragic
death of Private Hoskins' mother.

Remembering what the chaplain had said, the
sergeant-major decided to summon up all his reserves of
tact. When parade was over, he shouted to the company:

'All those with mothers, dismiss! WHERE DO YOU
THINK YOU'RE GOING, HOSKINS?'

186 The inscription on the gravestone read:
'Here lies a Justice of the Peace and an honest man.'

The passer-by commented: 'I wonder how they got
the two men into the same grave.'

187 On his death-bed poor Lubin lies;
    His spouse is in despair;
With frequent sobs and mutual cries,
    They both express their care.

'A different cause,' says Parson Sly,
    'The same effect may give:
Poor Lubin fears that he may die;
    His wife that he may live.'

(Matthew Prior)

188 Mr Glenn Gilheath from Chicago, on trial for his thirteenth robbery charge, aged seventy-two, said:

'Old burglars never die, they just steal away.'

189 A woman had fought a weight problem for years. She had tried 'The F-Plan', 'The Cambridge', 'The Hip and Thigh', 'The BBC' diets, she had spent months on health farms, years attending Weight Watchers—all to no avail. Finally she died, and her husband reverently placed her ashes in a small urn on the mantelpiece at home. Unfortunately, the urn was taken for an ashtray by a number of insensitive friends, but the husband was unaware of this until one of them looked at the urn and remarked:

'I see your wife is still putting on weight.'

190 Various last words are attributed to Lord Palmerston. The most famous are: 'Die, my dear doctor? That's the last thing I shall do.'

191 However, I prefer the even more confident exit line: 'I think I feel a little better.'

192 Lord Palmerston's confidence was nothing compared to a contemporary of his—a Union General in the American Civil War. The general was unsurpassed in his knowledge of ballistics. He pointed to some snipers far away and declared: 'They couldn't hit an elephant at this dist—'

193 Oscar Wilde kept his refined tastes to the last. Surveying the miserable decor of his room, he murmured: 'Either that wallpaper goes or I do.'

194 The prize for the most ironic death goes to Calchas the Soothsayer. A rival fortune teller predicted the hour of his death.

Calchas was furious and proudly sat through the appointed hour, counting the minutes. When the hour had passed and he was still alive, Calchas found the failure of his rival hilarious—and he died laughing.

195 A vicar had been plagued for many years by a con-man, who turned up at every opportunity with a different tale of woe. He had an incurable disease, his wife had left him, his children needed new shoes—could the vicar lend him a few pounds? Or, he was still dangerously ill and now his house had been burgled and it was uninsured because of a mix-up by the insurance people, could the vicar forward a little money until the crisis was over?

On and on the stories went, his fatal illness becoming increasingly terminal, yet somehow he managed to turn up on Christmas Eve the following year, or Good Friday, or in the middle of the church's gift day. He had an uncanny knack of finding the vicar at his most public and vulnerable moments. The good-natured vicar continued to support the old rogue until the man did, in fact, die— of an incurable disease known as Walking Drunkenly into a Bus.

The vicar arranged the funeral and when it came to the question of a tombstone, the stonemason was at a loss.

'May I suggest,' said the vicar, his Christian charity deserting him for a moment, 'something very, very heavy indeed?'

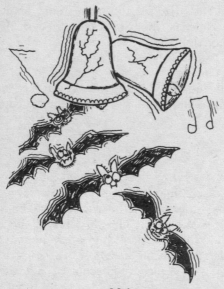

DIVINE
COMEDIES

In the television age the 'man in the street' has become an expert on every subject. One moment he is pushing a trolley of groceries out of Safeways, the next a microphone is thrust under his nose and he is asked to give his view on the hole in the ozone layer, the likely winner of the Vale of Glamorgan by-election or the existence of God. Awkward questions, when you're parked on a double-yellow line.

I think the most profound comment about religion ever given under these exacting conditions, was by the woman who said:

196 'I believe in heaven and hell but not in the afterlife.'

To be fair, the afterlife is a very tricky subject. The only people who can talk from experience of the matter are dead. So for those of us still alive, it leaves room for a lot of guesswork...and a lot of surprises.

197 A beautiful blonde actress arrived in heaven. St Cedric, who was reception that decade, was extremely surprised to see her—considering her infamous reputation on earth.

'Are you sure you've come to the right place?' he asked. The actress smiled seductively.

'I went to an evangelistic rally, where I was converted just before I died.'

'Those rallies are going too far these days,' murmured the dour old man. 'Life was much tougher in my day. Very well...but you'll have to walk ahead of me down that long corridor into heaven—and if you have one single naughty thought, a trap-door will open and you'll drop down to the other place.'

So the actress walked off down the corridor, swaying her hips. About halfway along, a trap-door opened and St Cedric fell through.

198 It was a cold winter's morning and the bishop stood by the roaring log fire in his palace. His first son, a rural dean, came down for breakfast.

'Good morning!' said the bishop. 'How did you sleep?'

'Very well, Father. In fact, I dreamt of heaven.'

'Really? And what was it like?'

'Wonderful! Just like home!'

The bishop gave him a kindly smile and the two men

stood by the fire, warming themselves. Soon, the second son — a canon — arrived.

'Good morning!' the bishop greeted him. 'Sleep well?'

'Marvellous, Father,' said the canon. 'I dreamt of heaven!'

'You too?' laughed the bishop. 'And what was it like?'

'Wonderful! Just like home!'

After many more minutes, the third and youngest son arrived, bleary-eyed. He was the black sheep of the family, an actor and a deep disappointment to his father.

'How did you sleep, my boy?' asked the bishop.

'Dreadful,' replied the youngest son. 'I dreamt of hell.'

'Oh dear!' said the bishop. 'What was it like?'

'Just like home. I couldn't get near the fire for all the clergy.'

199 Author writing on reincarnation invites letters from those with personal experience of same.

(*Advert in* Daily Telegraph)

200 The father was going out for the evening and leaving his little son in the care of a friend. The boy cried, begging his father to take him too.

'No,' said the father, firmly, 'stay here and be a good boy.' The three-year-old shouted and screamed and hurled his toys across the room. In desperation, the embarrassed father hissed:

'Listen, if you go on like that, you won't go to heaven when you die!'

'I don't want to go to heaven when I die!' screamed the boy. The father was nonplussed.

'You don't want to go to heaven?'

'No! I want to go with *you*, Daddy.'

201 A visitor arrived at a well-known Pentecostal church. It was packed and the place was buzzing with fervour, praise and rededication to God. The congregation sang forty-seven choruses—and that was before the service began. Afterwards, they sang the same forty-seven, repeating each one three times, increasing the volume. The preacher whipped up the people with shouts of 'Praise God!' and 'Thank you, Lord!' Finally, after a thundering sermon on Revelation 21, he shouted:

'Stand up all those who want to go to heaven!' Everyone stood. Except, that is, for the visitor, who soon became the focus of intense concern.

Loving hands were placed on his shoulders. People sighed in prayer, some cried, some smiled with confidence that he would know the joy of the Lord.

The preacher bore down upon him:

'Don't you want to go to heaven?' he boomed. To which the visitor replied:

'Not immediately.'

202 The bell rang loudly in heaven. St Peter opened the great pearly gates but there was no one there.

'Who was it?' asked Gabriel.

'Oh,' sighed St Peter, 'probably just agnostics ringing the doorbell again.'

203 An atheist was lying in the funeral parlour. The mortician put the finishing touches to the body and sighed.

'Look at him—all dressed up and nowhere to go.'

204 A man arrived at heaven's gate and was asked sternly if he had anything on his conscience. The man looked down, sorrowfully.

'I'm—afraid I have,' he stammered. 'You see—for years I've been—cheating.'

'Cheating?'

'I'm afraid so.'

'That's extremely serious.'

The man looked hopelessly at the locked gates.

'Go on.'

'Well, I was the scorer for the St Tudwal's darts team and every match I just added a few points, here and there, to our score and—that's how St Tudwal's became top of the Pub Darts League for five years running.'

'I don't think that's anything to worry about,' said the man with the white beard, opening the pearly gates. 'Come on in, lad.'

The man was overwhelmed.

'But St Peter, I thought—'

'Oh, I'm not St Peter,' said the kindly old man. 'He's got a day off. I'm St Tudwal.'

205 A pretty young convert was speaking at an evangelistic meeting: 'When I realised that my jewellery was dragging me down to hell, I gave it to my sister.'

LIFE
AND
SOUL

My favourite stage direction is in Shakespeare's A Winter's Tale: *'Exit pursued by a bear'. This is how a playwright, with a few deft strokes of the pen, can give a director a nervous breakdown—not only has he got to find a bear, but also about thirty-five understudies for the actor. A story, perhaps inspired by Shakespeare, goes like this:*

206 Two men are running furiously but a grizzly bear is about one hundred yards behind and gaining. Suddenly, one of the men stops and puts on a pair of running shoes.

'You're crazy,' shouts the other man, 'those won't help you outrun the bear!'

'All I have to do,' smiles his friend, catching him up, 'is outrun you.'

This perfectly illustrates the opposite principle to the sacrificial Christian life: self-preservation at all costs. And no one has ever parodied that position better than a former leader of the Liberal Party:

207 When Harold Macmillan ruthlessly purged the Tory cabinet in 1962, Jeremy Thorpe drily observed: 'No greater love hath a man than this, that he lay down his friends for his life.'

Here are some stories on the theme of the spiritual life, ranging from piety to palmistry to pastors, poetry and parachutes...

208 A mother was convinced that her wayward son would become a Christian. She lost no opportunity in telling him that one day he would come to the faith. She pleaded with him to mend his ways, to see the light; she sent him little cards with Bible verses on, spiritual books, tapes of powerful sermons, all to no avail. One day, she fell on her knees and prayed fervently that God would totally remove the obstacle to her son's conversion. There was a blinding flash and she vanished.

209 An incident in a Brazilian football match graphically illustrated the point that while there is a time to be on our knees, there is also a time for action. International footballer Roberto Rivelino received the ball straight from the kick-off and drove a shot from the half-way line: the ball whizzed past the goalkeeper's ear while he was still on his knees in the goal mouth completing his pre-match devotions.

(From the Major Chuckle column, edited by John Dixon and first reported in The Book of Heroic Failures *by Stephen Pile, Futura Publications.)*

210 'Mummy, do all fairy-tales begin: "Once upon a time"?'

'No, darling, some of them begin: "When I became a Christian all my problems were over." '

211 A parachutist jumped from a plane, but when he pulled his rip-cord nothing happened. As he plummeted down, the thought came that all he could do was pray. He knew only one prayer, so he cried out in desperation, 'For what we are about to receive may the Lord make us truly thankful.'

A tree broke his fall, and miraculously he lived. His testimony was that he had been saved by grace alone.

(From the Major Chuckle column, edited by John Dixon, quoting the Pssst! column of The Baptist Times, *July 28th 1985.)*

212 An actress was obsessed with clairvoyancy, palmistry, astrology, psychometry—you name it, she had tried everything from phrenology to star charts.

'I'm falling in love again,' she confided in another actress, 'and I'm simply desperate to know how it will all turn out for me! Would you recommend that I see a palmist or a mind-reader?'

'You'd better go to a palmist,' said her friend. 'At least you know you've got a palm.'

213 Everard Feilding, a Catholic who became secretary of the Society for Psychical Research, brought his sense of humour to his many painstaking investigations. Thus, going one day for a seance with a medium who specialised in 'apports'—the sudden 'materialisation' of incongruous objects out of the void—he was asked to wait in her room where, getting bored, he pulled aside a curtain to look out of the window, and found a heap of prawns behind it.

He had in his pocket a knife and some pink baby ribbon. He cut the ribbon into lengths, and embellished each prawn with an elegant bow before returning it to the pile. They appeared later at the seance, when the medium claimed she had brought them from the sea by psychic means. What she thought of their new sashes is not on record.

(Renée Haynes, 'Through Psi to Faith'
in The Tablet)

214 A London City Missionary was visiting an 'awkward customer' at the top of a high-rise block of flats and was told to 'clear off'.

'I'm nearer to God than you up here,' he was told.

'It's attitude not altitude,' said the missionary, beating a hasty retreat.

215 A woman said to a portrait painter: 'I want you to do me justice!'

'Madam,' replied the artist, 'it's not justice you need, but mercy!'

216 The pastor came to visit a beautiful young woman who was ill.

'I've been praying for you every day,' he told her.

'Oh pastor,' she smiled sweetly, 'and all the time you knew I was on the phone.'

217 A little still she strove, and much repented, And whispering 'I will ne'er consent'— consented.

(Byron, Don Juan*)*

218 Two nuns were driving through the countryside when they ran out of petrol. They walked to a nearby farmhouse for help and the kindly farmer said that they could siphon some of the petrol from his tractor. However, they could not find anything in which to carry the petrol, until the father produced a battered old chamber pot. The nuns filled the pot with petrol, walked back to the car and began pouring it in.

A passing motorist, hardly believing what he saw, stopped and said, 'I don't agree with your religion, but I admire your faith.'

219 Teacher: What is cleanliness next to?
Boy: Impossible.

220 Billy Graham was walking along the road when a friend pointed out a drunk and observed cynically:

'There goes one of your converts.'

'It might be one of mine,' replied Billy Graham, 'but it's certainly not one of God's.'

221 Whenever God erects a house of prayer,
The Devil always builds a chapel there;
And 'twill be found, upon examination,
The latter has the largest congregation.
(Daniel Defoe, 'The True-Born Englishman')

222 A long time ago, a parson thought it polite to wait for the country squire before beginning the service in his village church. One Sunday, he forgot and began with the opening scripture:

'When the wicked man—'

'Stop!' shouted the church-warden. 'He hasn't come yet.'

223 If we all decided that we had enough food, our houses were big enough, our cars satisfactory and our clothes sufficient, our economic system would collapse tomorrow.

224 Computers are now compiling dictionaries. When asked to define the word 'family', one electronic brain came up with the suggestion:

'A band of self-seeking individuals loosely held together by the television set.'

225 Advice in a magazine: 'Choose your parents carefully.'

226 We all need to know that we're loved—and some lovers are almost neurotic in their need to hear the words 'I love you', over and over again—but one eighty-year-old husband put a higher premium on keeping his word. On the day of their golden wedding anniversary, his wife said to him:

'Why, in the last fifty years, have you never said, "I love you"?'

He answered, 'Did I say "I love you" on the day I asked you to be my wife?'

'Yes.'

'Well,' said the old man, 'when the position changes, I'll let you know.'

227 The Archdeacon of Stafford will protest to the Air Ministry about a jet aircraft which flew low over St Mary's Church yesterday, making inaudible his prayer for world peace.

(Daily Mail)

228 Robert Browning was asked the meaning of an obscure passage in his poem 'Sordello'. Browning replied:

'When I wrote that, God and I knew what it meant, but now God alone knows.'

229 The little church was packed to hear the new minister. He was a young man, fresh from theological college, and he climbed up into the pulpit, head high, proud to be giving his first sermon.

He began to deliver his stirring message, but gradually he realised that he was losing the attention of his congregation. Some fell asleep, others stared blankly, one or two got up and left. By the end of the sermon, he felt utterly humiliated and crept down from the pulpit a broken man.

Afterwards, a wise old man—one of the elders of the church—shook his head.

'My boy,' he said gently, 'if only you'd gone up into that pulpit as you came down, you'd have come down as you'd gone up.'

230 Onward, Christian soldiers,
Each to war resigned,
With the Cross of Jesus
Vaguely kept in mind.
(Paul Dehn, 'A Modern Hymnal' from
The Fern on the Rock, Collected Poems 1935–65,
published by Hamish Hamilton 1965)

231 The Christian life of some churchgoers is so inconspicuous that you'd think Christ commanded his followers to 'Go out into all the world, shut up and keep your heads down.'

232 This approach to life is perfectly illustrated by a police recruit's response to a problem set in a training exam. It read as follows:

'You are on the beat and you see two dogs fighting. The dogs knock a baby out of its pram, causing a car to swerve off the road, smashing into a grocer's shop. A pedestrian is seriously injured, but during the confusion a woman's bag is snatched, a crowd of onlookers chase after the thief and, in the huge build up of traffic, the ambulance is blocked from the victim of the crash.

State, in order of priority, your course of action.'

He replied: 'Take off uniform and mingle with crowd.'

233 Mick had been drinking all night. First, he stole Sean's packet of cigarettes, then he tried to get off with Paddy's girl-friend. There was a terrible fight. Suddenly, Father O'Reilly came round the corner.

'My boy,' he roared, tearing him away, 'you must learn to love your enemies.'

'Dat's de problem, Fader,' said Mick, 'me worst enemies are whiskey, tobacco and women—and oi love dem all...'

234 Faith can move mountains—she's a big girl.

(Graffiti)

235 An African preacher, speaking on the text, 'What shall it profit a man if he gain the whole world and lose his own soul', argued that people can lose their souls by being *too charitable*. His congregation were astonished, but he went on to explain:

'Many people attend church, hear the sermon and, as soon as the service is over, divide it among their fellows—this part for that man, and that verse for that woman, and such and such a warning for Mr X, and this particular challenge for Mrs X—on and on they go. In this way, they give away the whole sermon and keep none for themselves.'

EPILOGUE:
THE
OLD JOKE

236 One of the first religious jokes I ever heard was about the vicar who was proud of his beautiful sports car. One Sunday morning it was stolen and a battered old Morris Minor was left in its place. He was still so upset, during the morning service, that he announced the first hymn as:

'Crock of ages left for me.'

It was over thirty years ago I heard that and I fell off my pew laughing. I was six. I still fall off my pew laughing these days, but not at that particular old joke—in fact, mainly at the idea of certain clergymen reciting the creed and other comic absurdities. Yet, to be fair on the 'old' joke, even apparently recent jokes often have a long history, perhaps an ancient history. Jokes have been around as long as human beings, longer if one takes the view that angels enjoy a good laugh in heaven (while hell is a place of unrelenting seriousness); and religious jokes have delighted—and offended—people at least since the begin-

nings of organised faiths, with their rituals and hierarchies.

The Bible is an excellent place to begin when looking for examples of early religious jokes, but before offering an illustration it is worth saying something on the vexatious issue of 'offence' and 'taste' in religious humour. I was intrigued by the reaction of one or two Christian booksellers to Rolling in the Aisles, for instance. There were some (a tiny minority) who withdrew it from their shops because it was thought that one or two jokes—or perhaps many jokes?—were unsuitable for Christian ears. One bookseller returned his copies to the publishers, writing: 'Personally I found the book very funny, but I couldn't possibly let my customers see it.' I will always treasure that letter and the image it conjures up in my mind of a manager sneaking a copy of Rolling in the Aisles out of a brown envelope under the counter, sniggering, and then stuffing it away hurriedly at the first sight of a pious customer: 'Ah, good morning, madam—er— Bible notes, was it?'

But even with the Bible, one can't be quite sure it's suitable reading for sensitive religious folk. One could argue that the book of 1 Kings, for example, should be suppressed because it contains one of the earliest risqué religious jokes on record.

237 Elijah is taunting the prophets of Baal in the famous contest on Mount Carmel. Baal, supposedly a god, is nowhere to be seen and Elijah lets rip with his sarcasm.

'And at noon Elijah began to mock the prophets of Baal, saying: "Call him louder. After all, he is a god. Perhaps he is deep in thought, or *on the toilet*, or on a journey?" '

(1 Kings 18:27)

I am told by my former Hebrew tutor, John Goldingay, now Principal of St John's College, Nottingham, that this is an accurate translation from the original—but not, it may be noted, the one adopted in any English language version of the Bible that I have seen. Poor Elijah. Jokes were always vulnerable to censorship. Still, it's a small price to pay for making sure the Bible is still available on the open shelves of some Christian bookshops.

The difficulties of defining good taste, even among the most sober-minded Christians, is splendidly illustrated by the two organisations that wrote to the publishers of Rolling in the Aisles *listing the jokes they thought were unsuitable for Christian readership.*

The remarkable thing about these two lists is that they did not coincide in a single joke. Even if a definitive list of 'unsound' jokes could be agreed, the danger would be just the same as with the famous Papal Index.

238 Eventually, the story goes, the Roman Catholic authorities had to put the *Papal Index* itself onto the *Index*, because it became such popular reading.

Back now to the ancient history of religious humour. It wasn't just the men of biblical times, but also of the classical era, that appreciated a good joke on a serious subject.

239 I have always admired the reaction of the Greek philosopher Demonax to a mediocre poet, who proudly showed him verses 'composed for my own epitaph'.

'Marvellous,' said Demonax. 'I just can't wait to see it in position.'

One could scan the last two thousand years for jokes about death, the afterlife, morality, priests, prayer, virtues and vices, and find examples from every century of that broad term 'religious humour' (in my view almost a tautology, because humour and spiritual awareness are so closely linked: even humour which is not on religious subject matter may be religious in essence). There are few richer periods than the Middle Ages, with the hilarity of the Mystery Plays and, of course, the irreverent comedy of Chaucer's Canterbury Tales. *However, here are just a few tail-pieces from the past four centuries. Some of these could be retold in modern English (I have kept them here in their original form, as recorded in manuscripts at the University Library, Cambridge) and perhaps one or two are still going the rounds. As for the jokes I have heard over the years, including those elsewhere in this book, I wouldn't like to bet on any of them being purely contemporary. Someone probably told the original version to a chortling monk in the cloisters of a thirteenth-century Cistercian abbey. Yet the humour of a good joke is always fresh: and vintage, as in wine, can be a richness to be savoured.*

240 A certain curate, preaching on a time to his parishioners, said that our Lord with five loaves had fed five hundred persons. The clerk, hearing him fail, said softly in his ear:

'Sir, ye err, the gospel is five thousand.'

'Hold thy peace, fool,' said the curate, 'they will scarcely believe that they were five hundred.'

(Sixteenth century)

241 A Scot was a-preaching how that all men are one another's neighbour and brother in Christ:

'Even the Turk, the Jew, the Moor, the cannibal, the far Indian,' and then concluded:

'Yea, and the very Englishman is our neighbour too.'

(Sixteenth century)

242 A gentleman being at chapel, where a very dull sermon quickly dispersed the congregation, remarked that the clergyman had made a very moving sermon.

(Seventeenth century)

243 A traveller reported to be drowned, a friend of his being in company when the letter came that brought the first news of his death, fetched a deep sigh, saying:

'Peace be on his soul, for he is gone the way of all flesh.'

'Nay,' said one near, 'if he be drowned he is rather gone the way of all fish.'

(Seventeenth century)

244 From a sermon preached at Great St Mary's, Cambridge: This *dial* shows we must *die all*; yet notwithstanding *all houses* are turned into *ale houses*, our *paradise* into a *pair of dice*, our *marriage* into a *merry age*, our *matrimony* into a *matter of money*, our *divines* into *dry vines*. It was not so in the days of *Noah, ah no!*

(Seventeenth century)

245 A curate preaching to his parishioners of the Day of Judgement said:

'At that day Christ will say to me, "Curate, what hast thou done with my sheep?" I shall answer:

"Beasts thou gavest them to me and so I return them to thee." '

(Eighteenth century)

246 A clergyman was walking home with one of his elderly parishioners, during a cold winter spell, when it happened that the old gentleman fell on the ice. The clergyman, always one to draw a sermon from life, remarked sternly:

'Friend, sinners stand on slippery places.' The old man looked at him and replied:

'I see they do, but I can't.'

(Nineteenth century)

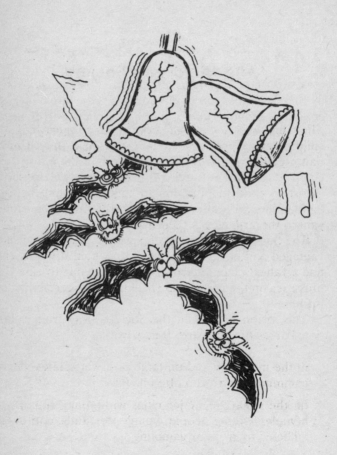

The Children's Society

The Children's Society has been working since 1881 for children and young people under pressure. As a Christian organisation (with special links with the Church of England and the Church in Wales) it works to show Christian concern in action to children, young people and families who often see the Christian faith as irrelevant to the struggles in their lives.

The Society has a vision of a society where the disadvantaged and devalued people with whom it works can find a valued place. It sees its role as helping to ease the pressures on their lives and speaking out where injustice is found.

This vision has taken the Society away from traditional areas of child care. It now works:

in the inner city and on large post-war estates where community spirit can often be low

on the streets of major cities with young runaways, homeless young people, young prostitutes and those addicted to drugs or gambling

with handicapped young people—fighting to keep them with their families and out of institutions with young people who have been in care—helping them to become independent without the support of their families

with parishes and other church groups—encouraging them to reach out to local children and families facing pressures.

The Society helps more than 11,000 children and young people every year through 126 projects in England and Wales.

INDEX

Figures indicate the joke number

151

Life And Other Problems

by Veronica Zundel

'If you have ever got up in the morning, dropped your radio in the bath and a full teacup in your handbag, or anything similar, we probably have a few things in common.'

This witty, wise and compassionate collection from Veronica Zundel's columns in *Christian Woman* brings together her sharpest, sanest observations on the pains and pleasures of life. Seeking to be 'entertaining, thought-provoking and not too religious', she writes on singleness, men, living in London, how not to get up in the morning, faith and free-style dancing. The results are cheerful and unpredictable, like an exploding box of fireworks.

VERONICA ZUNDEL grew up in Coventry and studied English at Oxford. She currently works as an editor at *Third Way* magazine and is a regular contributor to Scripture Union's *Alive to God* and *Daily Notes*. In 1983 she won the Magazine Publishing Award for Best Specialist Columnist for her columns in *Christian Woman*. She lives in central London with a 'small but refined' bear called Bertie.

Minstrel
Monarch Publications

Joan 'N' The Whale

by John Duckworth

These fresh and funny parables will make you think about your faith. John Duckworth uses humour, satire and fantasy to offer food for thought on living the Christian life. Cheerful and memorable, his stories hang in the mind. Ideal for the young and the young at heart.

Mad scientist Dr Emil Van Gelical creates 'Christianstein', the greatest specimen of spiritual life the world has ever known, but forgets one crucial ingredient.

After an audit by the Eternal Revenue Service, Mr Carper realises he didn't pay enough thanks.

When a young man calls at a clothes shop to purchase the whole armour of God, he is offered the Sash of Sincerity, the Sports Shirt of Niceness and the Hairspray of Holiness.

'Crackles with inventiveness... very, very funny indeed.' ADRIAN PLASS

Minstrel
Monarch Publications